Tricky, Sticky Bible Riddles

Grades 2–3

by Becky White

Carson-Dellosa Christian Publishing
Greensboro, North Carolina

Credits

It is the mission of Carson-Dellosa Christian Publishing to create the highest-quality Scripture-based children's products that teach the Word of God, share His love and goodness, assist in faith development, and glorify His Son, Jesus Christ.

". . . teach me your ways so I may know you. . . ."
Exodus 33:13

Editors .... Sabena Maiden, Pamela Holley–Bright
Layout Design .... Mark Conrad
Inside Illustrations.... Scott Burroughs
Cover Design .... Peggy Jackson
Cover Illustration...... Scott Burroughs

Scripture taken from the HOLY BIBLE, NEW INTERNATIONAL VERSION®. Copyright © 1973, 1978, 1984 by International Bible Society. Used by permission of Zondervan Bible Publishers.

ISBN: 978-1-59441-290-5

Table of Contents

How to Use This Book

Tricky, Sticky Bible Riddles contains 36 riddle pages and 36 corresponding puzzle pages. You may use the lessons in order or choose the riddles that best supplement your current curriculum (see page 3).

Quiz the class by reading the riddles, clues, and then the bonus questions. The first clue is tricky; clues two, three, and four are progressively easier. Pause after each clue to allow children to discuss or guess the answer. You may choose to allow children to refer to their Bibles during the clues. The fifth clue provides the Scripture reference that will solve the riddle.

Bonus and discussion questions follow each riddle. Read the Bible story to the class and then ask the questions. You may choose to share the provided Bible references if children need help with the answers. A prayer is provided to end each lesson with power!

Each riddle is followed by a reproducible puzzle page that reinforces the Bible lesson and adds more fun from God's Word!

Additional Ways to Play

Have a white- or chalkboard on hand to keep score when needed and a stopwatch if you choose to time children. Below are some additional ways to play the game.

Got a Clue?

1. One child is elected to go first.
2. The child selects a category: *Who? What? Where? or Why?*
3. The moderator reads the riddle aloud and sets a stopwatch for one minute.

4. If the child can answer the riddle before the end of one minute without any clues, he receives ten points.
5. If he cannot solve the riddle, he is then given five minutes. At any time the child may ask for a clue. For each clue given, the number of points awarded for the correct answer is reduced by one point. For example, the first clue is worth nine points, the second clue is worth eight points, etc.
6. While the child tries to answer, other children may use their Bibles to search for the answer. If the child cannot solve the riddle at the end of five minutes, the other children get a chance to answer for two points.
7. After each child has had an equal number of opportunities, the child with the most points is declared the winner.

Quizzical Question Challenge

1. Read the Bible story to the children.
2. Read the Bonus Question and set a stopwatch for one minute.
3. Children write their answers on a sheet of paper. Each correct answer is worth 10 points.
4. Read each discussion question (five points) and set a stop watch for one minute each. Provide the Scripture reference and allow children to look up the answers if necessary.

    ♦ For an extra challenge, allow children to make up their own Scripture-related questions and pose them to the other children.

CD-204023 *Tricky, Sticky Bible Riddles 2–3*

Road to 100

1. Read the riddle aloud and set a stopwatch for one minute. Announce that the solution is worth 100 points.

2. List each child's name and guess on a board without indicating if the riddle has been answered correctly.

3. Read the first clue, then give children one minute to answer.

4. List the guesses on the board.

5. Continue to read the clues.

6. After the first four clues have been given, read the last clue, which is the related Scripture reference, and give the answer.

7. Pose the bonus question and award 15 points to each child who answers correctly.

8. Calculate the scores to decide the winners.

Bean Business

This game offers an opportunity for all the riddles to be reviewed after they have been learned in class. It requires 36 index cards, a small container, and a bag of dried beans. Photocopy and then cut out the riddle portion of each riddle page and attach to the front of an index card. Cut out and attach the clues to the back of the corresponding index card. Make 36 game cards.

1. Each player is given 20 beans. The rest are placed in a container.

2. One player is elected to go first.

3. The first player shuffles the cards and places them with the clues side facedown.

4. Then, she draws the top card and reads the riddle aloud. If the player can solve the riddle, she gets 20 beans. If she offers an incorrect answer, she must place 10 beans in the container.

5. If the player cannot solve the riddle, she has two choices:

    ◆ She can buy as many clues (up to five) as she thinks she will need to solve the riddle. Each clue costs two beans. The player must say how many clues she wants to buy before being given the clues; she cannot buy them one at a time. The person to the right of player flips the card over and reads aloud the appropriate number of clues. The correct answer is still worth 20 beans.

    ◆ Or, she can challenge her neighbor—the player to her right. If he answers correctly, the neighbor receives 10 beans. If he answers incorrectly, he loses five beans.

6. After answering all 36 cards, the player with the most beans is the winner.

CD-204023 *Tricky, Sticky Bible Riddles 2–3*

Riddle #1

Man Saved Many

The Riddle

With God's help (and some creatures), this man saved his family, his friends, and many others. Who used different creatures to save many people?

The Clues

It happened in Egypt.

The man had a brother who sometimes helped him.

God used this man to send plagues upon the enemies of His people.

The man told Pharaoh many times to let his people go.

Exodus 12:31

The Solution

Moses *During the night Pharaoh summoned Moses and Aaron and said, "Up! Leave my people, you and the Israelites! Go, worship the LORD as you have requested."* Exodus 12:31

Bonus Question: What five different kinds of creatures did God use as plagues on Egypt?

Bonus Answer: *frogs, gnats, flies, livestock, and locusts*

Bible Story: Exodus 8, 9:1–12, 10

Discussion Questions:

1. Who was Moses' brother who sometimes helped him? (Exodus 7:1)
   Aaron

2. The second plague involved what kind of creatures? (Exodus 8:5)
   frogs

3. How did God use livestock as a punishment on the Egyptians? (Exodus 9:6)
   The livestock died.

The Prayer: Thank You, Lord, for our free country where we are not slaves. Thank You for giving us comfort when we are afraid and need strength. Thank You for hearing and answering our prayers. Amen.

CD-204023 *Tricky, Sticky Bible Riddles 2–3*

Then the LORD said to Moses, "Go to Pharaoh, for I have hardened his heart and the hearts of his officials so that I may perform these miraculous signs of mine among them . . ." Exodus 10:1

Directions: Decode the rest of the message to discover what God told Moses about the plagues. Check your answer by reading Exodus 10:2.

T   H   Y   R   M

 a  ou ay

_____   _____   _____

know  a I

_____   _____   ___

a e Lod.

_____   _____   _____

Riddle #2

Breakfast Is Served

The Riddle

This group of hungry people found nourishment in an unusual way. Who were the hungry people?

The Clues

This miracle happened to these people in the Desert of Sin.

The people complained to Moses and Aaron.

They saw the glory of the Lord appear in a cloud.

The Lord provided them with bread.

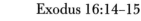
Exodus 16:14–15

The Solution

The Israelites *When the dew was gone, thin flakes like frost on the ground appeared on the desert floor. When the Israelites saw it, they said to each other, "What is it?" For they did not know what it was. Moses said to them, "It is the bread the LORD has given you to eat...."* Exodus 16:14–15

Bonus Question: Besides bread, what kind of food did God provide to the Israelites in the desert? (Exodus 16:13)

Bonus Answer: *quail meat*

Bible Story: Exodus 16:1–16

Discussion Questions:

1. How long had the Israelites been gone from Egypt when God sent the bread? (Exodus 16:1)
   two months and 15 days

2. Whom did Moses say that the people were grumbling against? (Exodus 16:8)
   the Lord

3. When was the meat supposed to arrive? When was the bread supposed to arrive? (Exodus 16:12)
   the meat at twilight, the bread at morning

The Prayer: Thank You, God, for paying attention to our physical needs, as well as our spiritual needs. Help us to never be grumblers but to live with thanksgiving in our hearts. Help us to stay strong in our faith and love and praise You. Amen.

CD-204023 *Tricky, Sticky Bible Riddles 2–3*

Name: _____

. . . Moses said to them, "It is the bread the LORD has given you to eat." Exodus 16:15

Directions: Decode the message to discover how the Lord fed the Israelites. Check your answer by reading Exodus 16:13.

A   E   I   O   U

Th🥖t 🧁v🧁ning q🍞🥖🥐l
_____   _____   _____

c🥖m🧁 🥖nd c🍞v🧁r🧁d
_____   _____   _____

the c🥖mp, 🥖nd 🥐n the
_____   _____

m🍞rning th🧁r🧁 w🥖s
_____   _____   _____

🥖 l🥖yer 🍞f d🧁w
_____   _____   _____

🥖r🍞🍞nd the c🥖mp.
_____   _____   _____

CD-204023 *Tricky, Sticky Bible Riddles 2–3*

Man with a Boastful Plan

The Riddle

A very confident man had an idea of how he could end the war between the Israelites and the Philistines. His plan was carried out but in the end, it cost him his life. Who was killed trying to carry out his plan?

The Clues

The man was from Gath.

The man yelled, "This day I defy the ranks of Israel!"

The man wore a bronze helmet and bronze armor.

The man was more than nine feet tall.

1 Samuel 17:8–9

The Solution

Goliath *Goliath stood and shouted . . . "Choose a man and have him come down to me. If he is able to fight and kill me, we will become your subjects; but if I overcome him and kill him, you will become our subjects and serve us."*
1 Samuel 17:8–9

Bonus Question: Who took the life of Goliath? (1 Samuel 17:50)

Bonus Answer: *David*

Bible Story: 1 Samuel 17:1–50

Discussion Questions:

1. Why did David go to the Valley of Elah where the men were fighting? (1 Samuel 17:17–18)
   He went to see how his brothers were doing and to get news from them. David's father also sent him to take food to the men.

2. What did David say to convince King Saul that he could fight the giant? (1 Samuel 17:34–37)
   He killed both a lion and a bear when he was keeping his father's sheep.

3. To whom did David say the battle belonged? (1 Samuel 17:47)
   the Lord

The Prayer: Thank You, God, for watching over all of us. Help us to remember that even when we are small, like David, we can do great things and good deeds in Your name. Amen.

CD-204023 *Tricky, Sticky Bible Riddles 2–3*

Name:

David said to the Philistine, "You come against me with sword and spear and javelin, but I come against you in the name of the LORD Almighty, the God of the armies of Israel, whom you have defied."
1 Samuel 17:45

Directions: Follow the directions below to reveal what David said to Goliath about the battle that they were getting ready to fight. Check your answer by reading 1 Samuel 17:47.

5 = A	16 = O	2, 13 = H	3, 9, 14 = E
4 = B	17 = R	8, 15 = L	1, 6, 7, 12 = T
18 = D	10 = I	11, 19 = S	

___ ___ ___ ___ ___ ___ ___ ___ ___
1   2   3   4   5   6   7   8   9

___ ___ ___ ___ ___ ___ ___ ___ ___ ___ , ...
10 11   12 13 14   15 16 17 18 19

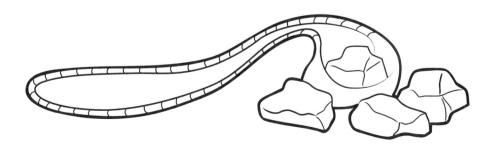

A King-Size Challenge

Riddle #4

The Riddle

Two arguing women challenged this man's wisdom. He quickly offered a strange solution and brought out the truth. Who settled the very difficult dispute between the two women?

The Clues

Two women were fighting over a baby.

One woman fought for the child's life.

The man was a king.

The king determined the child's true mother with his unusual solution.

1 Kings 3:27

The Solution

King Solomon *Then the king gave his ruling: "Give the living baby to the first woman. Do not kill him; she is his mother." 1 Kings 3:27*

Bonus Question: How did the people of Israel react to the king's verdict? (1 Kings 3:28)

Bonus Answer: *They were in awe of his God-given wisdom.*

Bible Story: 1 Kings 3:16–28

Discussion Questions:

1. What was the profession of the two women who were having the dispute? (1 Kings 3:16)
They were prostitutes.

2. Why were two women fighting over the same baby? (1 Kings 3:19–21)
One woman accidently killed her baby, so she stole the other woman's baby.

3. Why did King Solomon threaten to cut the baby in half? (1 Kings 3:26)
He wanted to prove who the real mother of the living baby was.

The Prayer: Thank You, God, for being a just God. Help our leaders turn to You for wisdom to make good decisions. Help us to be wise, know the truth, and do good in Your name. Amen.

CD-204023 *Tricky, Sticky Bible Riddles 2–3*

Name:

When all Israel heard the verdict the king had given, they held the king in awe. . . . 1 Kings 3:28

Directions: Decode the message to discover why the people held King Solomon in awe. Check your answer by reading 1 Kings 3:28.

E   S   I   M   H   A

...b [E] c [A] u [S] [E]   t [H] [E] y   [S] [A] w

_____   _____   _____

t [H] [A] t   [H] [E]   [H] [A] d

_____   _____

w [I] [S] do [M]   fro [M]   God

_____   _____   _____

to   [A] d [M] [I] n [I] [S] t [E] r

__   _____

ju [S] t [I] c [E] .

_____

A Whirlwind Experience

Riddle #5

Who

The Riddle

While two friends took a walk, one was swept up in a sudden blaze, never to be seen again. Who was the man who disappeared in the fiery scene?

The Clues

Just before the man disappeared, he and his friend had crossed the Jordan River on dry land.

One man thought that the other would be leaving him soon.

A horse and chariot showed up.

The man who disappeared was taken to heaven in a whirlwind.

2 Kings 2:11, 17

The Solution

Elijah *As they were walking along and talking together, suddenly a chariot of fire and horses of fire appeared and separated the two of them, and Elijah went up to heaven in a whirlwind. . . . And they sent fifty men, who searched for three days but did not find him.*
2 Kings 2:11, 17

Bonus Question: Who was with Elijah when he disappeared? (2 Kings 2:11–12)

Bonus Answer: *Elisha*

Bible Story: 2 Kings 2:1–18

Discussion Questions:

1. What did Elisha ask Elijah to give him? (2 Kings 2:9)
   a double portion of his spirit

2. Immediately after Elijah disappeared, what did Elisha do to his own clothes? (2 Kings 2:12)
   He tore them apart.

3. What did Elisha do to Elijah's cloak? (2 Kings 2:14)
   He struck the water with it.

The Prayer: Lord, thank You for our friends—especially our Christian friends whom we can support and with whom we can build our faith together. Help us to demonstrate the qualities of good friendship the way that Elisha and Elijah did. Amen.

As they were walking along and talking together, suddenly a chariot of fire and horses of fire appeared and separated the two of them. . . . 2 Kings 2:11

Directions: Look up 2 Kings 2:12 to find the name Elisha called out when he saw the chariot of fire. Fit the name in the number-letter grid by following the directions below. The first letter has been done for you.

Letter 2: Connect E1 to E10. Connect E1 to H1. Connect H1 to H10. Connect E5 to H5.

Letter 3: Connect I1 to M1. Connect K1 to K10.

Letter 4: Connect N1 to N10. Connect Q1 to Q10. Connect N5 to Q5.

Letter 5: Connect R1 to R10. Connect R1 to U1. Connect R5 to U5. Connect R10 to U10.

Letter 6: Connect V1 to V10. Connect V1 to Z1. Connect Z1 to V5. Connect V5 to Z6. Connect Z6 to Z10.

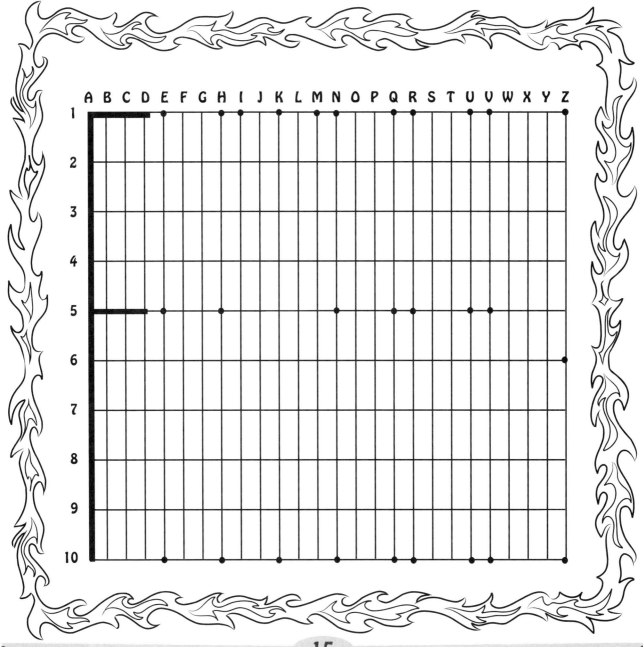

CD-204023 *Tricky, Sticky Bible Riddles 2–3*

Taunters Taught a Lesson

Riddle #6

The Riddle

This man, who was being insulted by a crowd, received help from a pair of cooperative animals. Who taught the crowd a lesson with the help of two animals?

The Clues

It happened near Bethel.

It involved a crowd of youths.

The taunters called the man a name.

The man called down a curse on them in the Lord's name.

2 Kings 2:23

The Solution

Elisha . . . *As he was walking along the road, some youths came out of the town and jeered at him. "Go on up, you baldhead!" they said. . . .*
2 Kings 2:23

Bonus Question: What animals aided Elisha? (2 Kings 2:24)

Bonus Answer: *two bears*

Bible Story: 2 Kings 2:19–25

Discussion Questions:

1. Just before the youths mocked Elisha, what miracle did he perform? (2 Kings 2:21)
   He healed the water.

2. How was the miracle performed? (2 Kings 2:20–22)
   Elisha threw the salt into the water.

3. What nickname did the jeering crowd call Elisha? (2 Kings 2:23)
   Baldhead

The Prayer: Heavenly Father, thank You for the Scriptures that share stories about Your people. Help us to never be like the youths who mocked Elisha. Let us always be reminded to honor all adults and never tease others. Amen.

Name:

And he went on to Mount Carmel and from there returned to Samaria. 2 Kings 2:25

Directions: Elisha traveled from Bethel to Mount Carmel and back to Samaria. Find the shortest route from Bethel to Mount Carmel to Samaria.

CD-204023 *Tricky, Sticky Bible Riddles 2–3*

Cousin Dunks Cousin

Riddle #7

The Riddle

When this young man intentionally pushed his cousin's head under water, he immediately heard from his cousin's father. Who dunked his cousin's head under water?

The Clues

It happened in the Jordan River.

The cousin asked to be dunked under water by him.

The "dunking" was a baptism.

God voiced his approval after the baptism.

Matthew 3:13

The Solution

Jesus' cousin, John the Baptist *Then Jesus came from Galilee to the Jordan to be baptized by John.* Matthew 3:13

Bonus Question: Who spoke to Jesus and John immediately after the baptism? (Matthew 3:16–17)

Bonus Answer: *God*

Bible Story: Matthew 3:13–17

Discussion Questions:

1. Where had Jesus been before arriving at the Jordan River? (Matthew 3:13)
   Galilee

2. What was John's reaction when Jesus asked to be baptized? (Matthew 3:14)
   John said, "I need to be baptized by you, and do you come to me?"

3. Before God spoke, what did they see? (Matthew 3:16)
   Heaven opened, and they saw the Spirit of God come down and land on Jesus.

The Prayer: Heavenly Father, thank You for our extended family members such as cousins, aunts, and uncles. Thank You for parents, grandparents, and other family members who love and support us. Thank You, Lord, for allowing us to be baptized like Jesus. We are glad to be Your children and a part of Your family. Amen.

CD-204023 *Tricky, Sticky Bible Riddles 2–3*

As soon as Jesus was baptized, he went up out of the water. At that moment heaven was opened, and he saw the Spirit of God descending like a dove and lighting on him. Matthew 3:16

Directions: Cross out every other letter to uncover what the voice from heaven said. The first one has been done for you. Check your answer by reading Matthew 3:17.

ANSWER:

T̶E̶H̶B̶I̶X̶S̶A̶   THIS

IVSE   _____

MAYT   _____

STOENE   _____ ,

WLHEOBME   _____

IM   _____

LBOEVWET   _____ ;

WTIETOHP   _____

HRINME   _____

IT   _____

ABME   _____

WTEXLELE   _____

PTLBEEAZSSEEDT.   _____ .

CD-204023 *Tricky, Sticky Bible Riddles 2–3*

Help from a Stranger

The Riddle

A sick woman touched a piece of fabric and was helped by this man, who was a complete stranger to her. Who was this helpful stranger?

The Clues

The woman had a serious health condition for 12 years.

The woman was in a large crowd.

The fabric that she touched was from the stranger's cloak.

The woman was healed because of her great faith.

Mark 5:27–29

The Solution

Jesus *When she heard about Jesus, she came up behind him in the crowd and touched his cloak, because she thought, "If I just touch his clothes, I will be healed." Immediately her bleeding stopped and she felt in her body that she was freed from her suffering.* Mark 5:27–29

Bonus Question: When the woman touched Jesus, what happened to Him? (Mark 5:30)

Bonus Answer: *He knew that power had gone out of Him.*

Bible Story: Mark 5:25–34

Discussion Questions:

1. Who was with Jesus when the woman touched Him? (Mark 5:31)
   the disciples and a large crowd

2. What did the woman do when Jesus asked who had touched Him? (Mark 5:33)
   She fell to His feet and told Him the truth about everything.

3. What did Jesus say to the woman about her faith? (Mark 5:34)
   He said that her faith had healed her.

The Prayer: Dear God, help us to have strong faith, like the faith of the woman who was reaching out to Jesus. Thank You, Lord, for our good health and well-being. Amen.

CD-204023 *Tricky, Sticky Bible Riddles 2–3*

> Then the woman, knowing what had happened to her, came and fell at his feet and, trembling with fear, told him the whole truth. Mark 5:33

Directions: Look up Mark 5:34 to find out what Jesus gave to the woman. Fit the gift in the number-letter grid by following the directions below. The first letter has been done for you.

Letter 2: Connect F1 to F10. Connect F1 to J1. Connect F5 to J5. Connect F10 to J10.

Letter 3: Connect K1 to K10. Connect K1 to O1. Connect O1 to O10. Connect K5 to O5.

Letter 4: Connect Q1 to Q10. Connect Q1 to U2. Connect Q10 to U9.

Letter 5: Connect V1 to V10. Connect V1 to Z1. Connect V5 to Z5. Connect V10 to Z10.

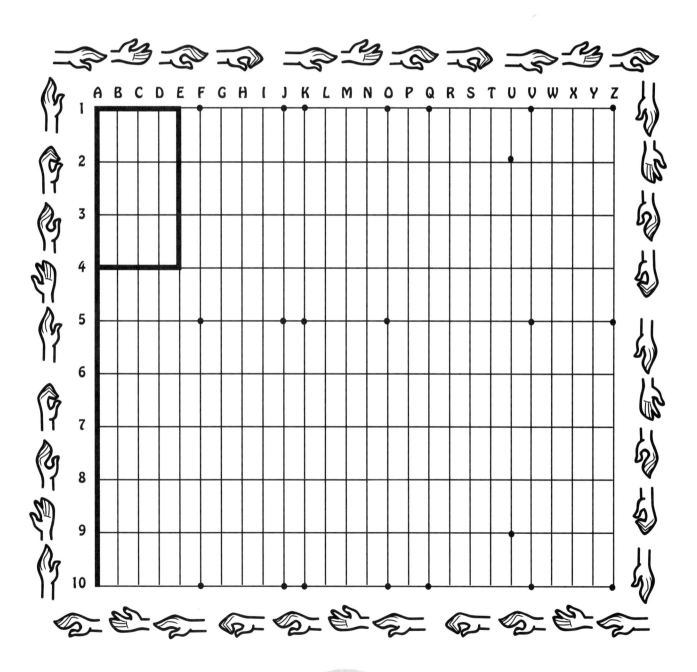

CD-204023 *Tricky, Sticky Bible Riddles 2–3*

Dousing the Dinner Guest

The Riddle

As some people were having dinner, this woman intentionally spilled something on one of her guests. Who spilled something on her dinner guest?

The Clues

It happened in Bethany.

The dinner was at Lazarus' home.

The guest of honor defended the woman's actions.

The spilled liquid was expensive perfume.

John 12:3

The Solution

Mary *Then Mary took about a pint of pure nard, an expensive perfume; she poured it on Jesus' feet and wiped his feet with her hair. And the house was filled with the fragrance of the perfume.* John 12:3

Bonus Question: Who was the guest of honor at the dinner? (John 12:2)

Bonus Answer: *Jesus*

Bible Story: John 12:1–11

Discussion Questions:

1. What were the names of Mary's sister and brother? (John 12:2)
   Martha and Lazarus

2. A large crowd had gathered to see Jesus and someone else. Whom did the people want to see? (John 12:9)
   Lazarus

3. Why did the chief priests make plans to kill Lazarus as well as Jesus? (John 12:10–11)
   Jesus raised Lazarus from the dead, so the people were putting their faith in Jesus instead of in the priests.

The Prayer: Heavenly Father, thank You, for sending Jesus to earth to die for our sins. Thank You for His example of how to love others. Help us remember to love others the way that Jesus loved His disciples, His friends, and even His enemies. Amen.

CD-204023 *Tricky, Sticky Bible Riddles 2–3*

Who Riddle #9

Name: _____

"Why wasn't this perfume sold and the money given to the poor? It was worth a year's wages." John 12:5

Directions:

1. Photocopy this page.
2. Cut along the solid lines to cut out the scripture mat and word strips.
3. Fold the mat in half horizontally, centering the dotted lines. Cut a slit along each dotted line.
4. Weave the word strips together to see Jesus' response to Judas's question.

Scripture Mat

	"You		always		the
poor		you,		you	
	always		me."		John 12:8

Word Strips

will	have

among	but	will

not	have

23

Riddle #1

The Riddle

A young couple did something simple that cost them their luxurious lifestyle. What did the wife and husband do that cost them their way of life?

The Clues

It was a tasty mistake.

The wife followed bad advice.

She thought that she would become wise if she took the advice.

The woman gave something to her husband.

Genesis 3:6

The Solution

They disobeyed God by eating from the Tree of Knowledge. *When the woman saw that the fruit of the tree was good for food and pleasing to the eye, and also desirable for gaining wisdom, she took some and ate it. She also gave some to her husband, who was with her, and he ate it.* Genesis 3:6

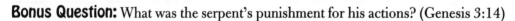

Bonus Question: What was the serpent's punishment for his actions? (Genesis 3:14)

Bonus Answer: *He was cursed to crawl on his belly and eat dust all of the days of his life.*

Bible Story: Genesis 3:1–24

Discussion Questions:

1. What did Eve tell the serpent about the tree in the middle of the garden? (Genesis 3:3)
   If she ate from the tree, she would die.

2. What did the serpent tell Eve about eating from the tree? (Genesis 3:4–5)
   She wouldn't die, but she would know both good and evil.

3. What excuse did Adam give to God for eating the forbidden fruit? (Genesis 3:12)
   The woman that God gave Adam made him eat the fruit.

The Prayer: Lord, thank You, for teaching us right from wrong. Thank You for the Bible, Your Word, which tells us how to live. Help us to be obedient to You. Amen.

 CD-204023 *Tricky, Sticky Bible Riddles 2–3*

Name:

To Adam he said, "Because you listened to your wife and ate from the tree about which I commanded you, 'You must not eat of it' . . . . Genesis 3:17

Directions: Follow the directions below to reveal what God told Adam. Check your answer by reading Genesis 3:17.

1. Change all of the Js to As.
2. Change all of the Ks to Es.
3. Change all of the Qs to Is.
4. Change all of the Vs to Os.
5. Change all of the Xs to Us.
6. Fill in the remaining letters.

Cxrskd   qs   thk   grvxnd

_____ ____ ____ _____

bkcjxsk   vf   yvx;   thrvxgh

_____ ____ ____ _____

pjqnfxl   tvql   yvx   wqll

_____ ____ ____ ____

kjt   vf   qt   jll   thk

____ ____ ____ ____ ____

djys   vf   yvxr   lqfk.

____ ____ ____ ____

CD-204023 *Tricky, Sticky Bible Riddles 2–3*

Riddle #2

An Unbroken Record

The Riddle

Noah's grandfather holds a record that has never been broken. What amazing record did Noah's grandfather set?

The Clues

When Enoch was 65 years old, he became the father of Methuselah.

When Methuselah was 187 years old, he became the father of Lamech.

Lamech was 182 years old when he had a son named Noah.

Methuselah's name is sometimes used to mean that something is very old.

Genesis 5:27

The Solution

Methuselah lived longer than any other human. *Altogether, Methuselah lived 969 years, and then he died.* Genesis 5:27

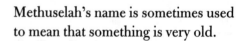

Bonus Question: Who were Methuselah's three great-grandsons? (Genesis 5:32)

Bonus Answer: *Noah's sons: Shem, Ham, and Japheth*

Bible Story: Genesis 5:21–32

Discussion Questions:

1. How long did Methuselah's father live? (Genesis 5:23)
   He lived 365 years.

2. What did Lamech say that his son would do? (Genesis 5:29)
   He would comfort them while they worked the land.

3. How much longer did Methuselah live than his father? (Genesis 5: 23, 27)
   He lived 604 more years than his father.

The Prayer: Thank You, God, for our eternal life with You. Help us to remember that this is not our only life—this is our earthly life. While we are on this earth, let us do what is good and righteous so that we will draw others to You. Amen.

CD-204023 *Tricky, Sticky Bible Riddles 2–3*

Name: _____

Altogether, Noah lived 950 years, and then he died. Genesis 9:29

Directions: Look up Genesis 5:1–32. Complete the family tree by filling in the life span of each of Noah's ancestors.

Adam lived _____ years.

Seth lived _____ years.

Enosh lived _____ years.

Kenan lived _____ years.

Mahalalel lived _____ years.

Jared lived _____ years.

Enoch lived _____ years.

Methuselah lived _____ years.

Lamech lived _____ years.

Noah lived 950 years.

Riddle #3

What

Man Goes to Mountaintop

The Riddle

A man reached the top of a mountain range without even climbing. What did the man use to reach the mountaintop?

The Clues

He was told exactly how to build it.

The man took his family on a trip.

It was raining on the day that they left for the trip.

The man took animals on the trip, too.

Genesis 8:4

The Solution

He used an ark. *And on the seventeenth day of the seventh month the ark came to rest on the mountains of Ararat.* Genesis 8:4

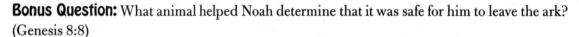

Bonus Question: What animal helped Noah determine that it was safe for him to leave the ark? (Genesis 8:8)

Bonus Answer: *a dove*

Bible Story: Genesis 8

Discussion Questions:

1. What was the first creature to leave the ark? (Genesis 8:6–7)
   a raven

2. When the earth was completely dry, what did God tell Noah to do? (Genesis 8:15–19)
   to release the animals

3. What did Noah do after God spoke to him? (Genesis 8:20)
   He built an altar and made a sacrifice to Him.

The Prayer: Dear Lord, Noah was a righteous man who followed your command. Help us to always put You first and to follow Your Word. Help us be righteous and strong in Your Name. Amen.

CD-204023 *Tricky, Sticky Bible Riddles 2–3*

Pairs of clean and unclean animals . . . came to Noah and entered the ark, as God had commanded Noah. Genesis 7:8–9

Directions: Find the three the animals in the puzzle that don't have mates.

The _____ does not have a mate.

The _____ does not have a mate.

The _____ does not have a mate.

Dangerous Dream

The Riddle

A boy dreamed about 13 things, and it nearly cost him his life. What were the 13 things that the boy dreamed about?

The Clues

 The boy who dreamed about the 13 things was 17 years old.

 The dreamer was envied by his brothers.

 The dreamer had a nice robe that was a gift from his father, Jacob.

 The dreamer was Joseph.

Genesis 37:9

The Solution

He dreamed of the sun, moon, and eleven stars. *Then he had another dream, and he told it to his brothers. "Listen," he said, "I had another dream, and this time the sun and moon and eleven stars were bowing down to me." Genesis 37:9*

Bonus Question: What price did Joseph pay for telling his brothers his dream? (Genesis 37:28)

Bonus Answer: *He was sold into slavery.*

Bible Story: Genesis 37

Discussion Questions:

1. Why were Joseph's brothers envious of him? (Genesis 37:3–4)
   His father loved him more than his brothers.

2. Which of Joseph's brothers did not want to kill him? (Genesis 37:21–22)
   Reuben

3. Which brother gave a suggestion that saved Joseph's life? (Genesis 37:26–27)
   Judah

The Prayer: Lord, we cannot know the future. When things happen, we don't always know why. Help us to be patient and trust You. Help us to love our brothers and sisters and not be jealous when good things happen to them. Amen.

CD-204023 *Tricky, Sticky Bible Riddles 2–3*

Name: _____

When he told his father as well as his brothers, his father rebuked him . . . ." Genesis 37:10

Directions: Decode the message to discover the question that Jacob asked his son about the dream. Check your answer by reading Genesis 37:10.

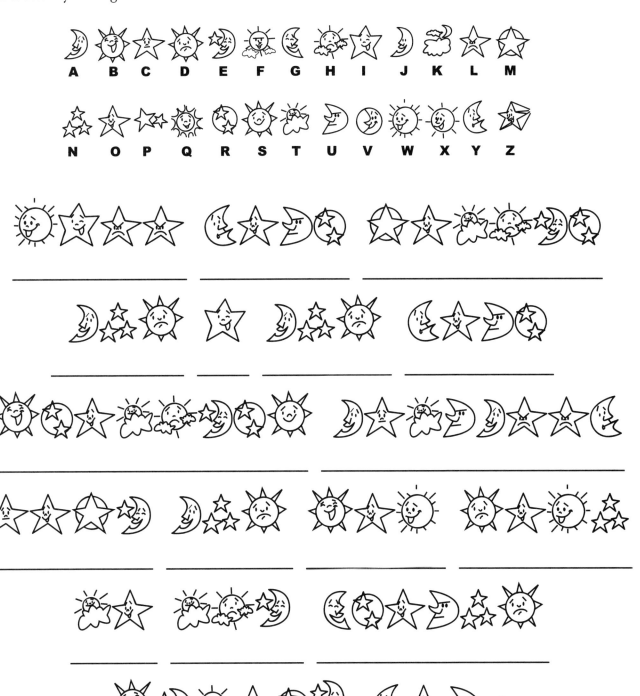

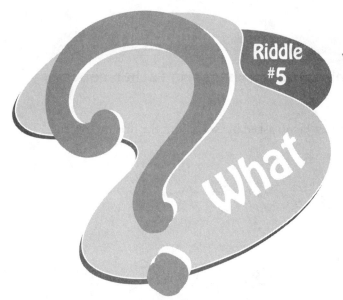

Meteorological Miracle

The Riddle

For those who survived a meteorological miracle, it was the longest day of their lives. What was the meteorological miracle?

The Clues

! It happened near Gilgal.

! After marching all night, an army took their foe by surprise.

! Joshua was the army's leader.

! The Lord listened to Joshua.

! Joshua 10:12–13

The Solution

The sun stopped in the middle of the sky. *On the day the L ORD gave the Amorites over to Israel, Joshua said to the L ORD in the presence of Israel: "O sun, stand still over Gibeon, O moon, over the Valley of Aijalon." So the sun stood still . . . The sun stopped in the middle of the sky and delayed going down about a full day.*
Joshua 10:12–13

Bonus Question: What other meteorological miracle did God perform to help Joshua win the battle? (Joshua 10:11)

Bonus Answer: *Hailstones fell on the Amorites.*

Bible Story: Joshua 10:7–15

Discussion Questions:

1. What did the Lord say to Joshua before the battle? (Joshua 10:8)
   to not be afraid, because no one would be able to withstand him

2. How long did the sun stand still? (Joshua 10:13)
   a full day

3. How did everyone know that the Lord was fighting for Israel? (Joshua 10:14)
   There was never a day like it before or after the battle.

The Prayer: Thank You, God, for the reassurance that You are always there watching out for us. Help us remember that You can always perform miracles for us. Amen.

CD-204023 *Tricky, Sticky Bible Riddles 2–3*

Name:

... The sun stopped in the middle of the sky and delayed going down about a full day. Joshua 10:13

Directions: Photocopy this page. Look up the verses from the Bible references given below. Then, cut and paste the appropriate weather stamp in each box.

Genesis 7:12	Psalm 93:4	Matthew 2:2	Genesis 1:14
Psalm 51:7	Psalm 104:4	Exodus 9:23	Psalm 104:3

33

Ghost on the Water

The Riddle

While some friends were in a little boat, they were suddenly terrified by what they thought was a ghost. What frightened the men?

The Clues

It was a windy evening.

The friends saw something coming toward them.

One man got out of the boat.

The wind died down after the men realized what had happened.

Matthew 14:25–27

The Solution

Jesus walked on water.
During the fourth watch of the night Jesus went out to them, walking on the lake. When the disciples saw him walking on the lake, they were terrified. "It's a ghost," they said, and cried out in fear. But Jesus immediately said to them: "Take courage! It is I. Don't be afraid." Matthew 14:25–27

Bonus Question: When Peter saw Jesus walking on the water, what did he say? (Matthew 14:28)

Bonus Answer: *"Lord, if it's you," Peter replied, "tell me to come to you on the water."*

Bible Story: Matthew 14:22–36

Discussion Questions:

1. What happened when Peter left the boat? (Matthew 14:29–30)
   He became afraid when he saw the wind.

2. What did Jesus do to help Peter? (Matthew 14:31)
   He reached out His hand and caught Peter.

3. When Jesus got into the boat, what did the disciples do? (Matthew 14:33)
   They worshiped Him.

The Prayer: Heavenly Father, help us to never doubt Your faithfulness. Help us to live lives that demonstrate to others that Your children are special and good. I love You, Lord. Amen.

34

Name: _____

Immediately Jesus reached out his hand and caught him. . . .
Matthew 14:31

Directions: Decode the message to discover the rest of the Scripture. Check your answer by reading Matthew 14:31.

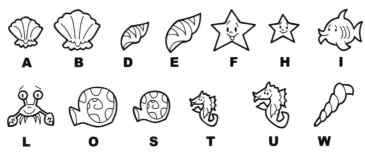

_____   _____   _____

_____   _____   _____

_____   _____   _____

_____

CD-204023 *Tricky, Sticky Bible Riddles 2–3*

Unidentified Falling Object

What

The Riddle

Pharisees and teachers of the law were listening to Jesus, when something landed in the middle of the crowd right in front of Jesus. It was so heavy that it could have injured someone. What object landed in front of Jesus?

The Clues

The power of the Lord was present.

Jesus said, "Friend, your sins are forgiven."

The object removed itself.

Jesus was praised for healing that day.

Luke 5:18–19

The Solution

A paralytic man on a mat landed in front of Jesus. *Some men came carrying a paralytic on a mat and tried to take him into the house to lay him before Jesus. When they could not find a way to do this because of the crowd, they went up on the roof and lowered him on his mat through the tiles into the middle of the crowd, right in front of Jesus. Luke 5:18–19*

Bonus Question: What did Jesus say to the paralytic man that angered the Pharisees? (Luke 5:20)

Bonus Answer: *"Friend, your sins are forgiven."*

Bible Story: Luke 5:17–26

Discussion Questions:

1. What did the Pharisees think when they heard Jesus tell the man that his sins were forgiven? (Luke 5:21) *They thought that it was blasphemy.*

2. When Jesus knew what the Pharisees were thinking, what did He ask them? (Luke 5:22–24) *"Which is easier: to say 'Your sins are forgiven,' or to say, 'Get up and walk' "?*

3. What happened when Jesus told the paralyzed man to get up and go home? (Luke 5:25) *He got up, took his mat, and went home praising God.*

The Prayer: Thank You, God, for our health and for the many abilities You have given us. Thank You also for Bible stories about Jesus and how He healed the sick. Help us to have faith as strong as the paralyzed man's faith that healed him. Amen.

"Everyone was amazed and gave praise to God. They were filled with awe and said. . . . Luke 5:26

Directions: Look up Luke 5:26. Find the word path that spells the rest of the Scripture verse, starting and ending where the arrows indicate. Words can be found by going left, right, up, down, and diagonally.

↓

"W	E	T	G	U	C	A	W	E	R	T	U	C	J
R	H	M	N	Y	R	D	A	Z	Q	T	M	Y	H
T	A	U	E	W	X	C	U	B	N	M	R	E	M
O	U	Y	S	R	E	W	Q	A	Z	X	C	B	N
P	M	N	E	E	U	C	X	Z	A	Q	W	E	R
N	M	P	L	N	R	E	O	K	A	I	U	Y	T
T	Y	E	D	C	A	M	A	R	B	L	Z	E	R
U	Y	G	J	K	L	R	T	Y	E	T	C	B	N
W	T	R	C	O	T	S	G	N	I	H	E	W	Q
M	S	Z	U	D	A	K	J	H	G	F	D	S	A
N	T	T	Y	N	Y." →								
U	R	F	T	B	U								
C	E	U	C	S	X								
X	D	I	U	R	Z								
A	Z	O	P	J	N								

Riddle #8

?What

The Riddle

A man went to great heights to get a better view. What did the man do to get a better look at what he wanted to see?

The Clues

! It happened in Jericho.

! The man was a wealthy tax collector.

! The man was short.

! Jesus told the man to come down.

! Luke 19:4

The Solution

Zacchaeus climbed a tree. *He wanted to see who Jesus was, but being a short man he could not, because of the crowd. So he ran ahead and climbed a sycamore-fig tree to see him, since Jesus was coming that way. Luke 19:3–4*

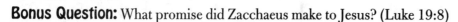

Bonus Question: What promise did Zacchaeus make to Jesus? (Luke 19:8)

Bonus Answer: *Zacchaeus promised to pay back anyone whom he had cheated four times the amount that he had taken.*

Bible Story: Luke 19:1–10

Discussion Questions:

1. Why couldn't Zacchaeus see Jesus? (Luke 19:3)
   He was a short man and couldn't see Jesus through the crowd.

2. When Jesus saw Zacchaeus in the tree, what did He tell him to do? (Luke 19:5)
   to come down from the tree

3. Why did the people think that Jesus shouldn't go to Zacchaeus' house? (Luke 19:7)
   Zacchaeus was a sinner.

The Prayer: Lord, help us to be honest in all of our dealings with others. If we have ever cheated somebody, help us make amends. Help us to not judge others but to be loving as Jesus was to all. Amen.

CD-204023 *Tricky, Sticky Bible Riddles 2–3*

Name: _____

Jesus said to him, "Today salvation has come to this house . . . ."
Luke 19:9

Directions: Look up Luke 19:9–10. Find the word path that spells the rest of the Jesus' words, starting and ending where the arrows indicate.

"B	E	C	C	A	N,	T	OO,	I	S	S	Z	R	
S	U	A	A	M	N	O	I	O	S	A	S	I	P
E	T	H	I	S	N	O	O	O	J	K	O	N	O
E	O	S	H	Y	F	M.	A	H	A	R	B	A	F
F	N	E	T	R	O	X	R	E	W	B	Y	U	I
A	O	F	M	A	N	R	E	T	O	S	R	R	O
A	E	Q	Z	M	C	A	M	R	T	E	E	K	A
K	F	S	A	O	Q	Y	B	E	U	L	L	D	N
T	G	E	Q	P	F	O	E	U	A	S	O	T	W
S	H	R	R	E	Z	H	W	D	B	M	F	D	W
T	J	T	T	R	A	A	P	O	O	Q	A	A	E
T	K	Y	Y	A	W	T	T						
Z	L	U	H	S	L	I	L						
L	M	I	E	U	O	S	T."						
O	B	O	W	J	R	M	X						
R	V	P	N	M	E	K	E						

CD-204023 *Tricky, Sticky Bible Riddles 2–3*

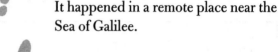

Hungry Crowd

What

The Riddle

A total stranger in a crowd took away a boy's possession, but the boy didn't seem to be bothered by this action. What was taken from the boy?

The Clues

It happened in a remote place near the Sea of Galilee.

A very large crowd had gathered.

The stranger who took the boy's possession was a disciple named Andrew.

Once taken, the boy's possession grew much bigger.

John 6:9

The Solution

The boy's lunch was taken. *"Here is a boy with five small barley loaves and two small fish, but how far will they go among so many?"* John 6:9

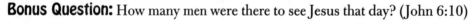

Bonus Question: How many men were there to see Jesus that day? (John 6:10)

Bonus Answer: *over 5,000 men*

Bible Story: John 6:1–14

Discussion Questions:

1. Why did Jesus ask, "Where shall we buy bread for these people to eat?" (John 6:5–6)
   to test Philip

2. How much food was in the boy's lunch? (John 6:9)
   five small barley loaves and two small fish

3. How much food was left after everyone had eaten? (John 6:13)
   There were 12 baskets filled with the leftover pieces from the five barley loaves.

The Prayer: Thank You, Lord, for the food that you provide. Thank You for sending Jesus, who showed us how to have eternal food. Help us remember that even small children can do mighty work in Your Name. Amen.

CD-204023 *Tricky, Sticky Bible Riddles 2–3*

Name:

"When Jesus looked up and saw a great crowd coming toward him, he said to Philip, "Where shall we buy bread for these people to eat?" John 6:5

Directions: Decode the message to discover what people said about the miracle. Check your answer by reading John 6:14.

C   E   L   M

O   P   S   T

_____ _____ _____

_____ _____

_____ _____ _____

_____ _____ .

CD-204023 *Tricky, Sticky Bible Riddles 2–3*

Nowhere to Run

The Riddle

A group of people were trapped between this large obstacle and a pursuing army. Just when all seemed lost, a force from the east saved the day. Where were the trapped people standing?

The Clues

The trapped people were once slaves.

The people questioned their leader for bringing them to this place.

The Lord made the wheels fall off the pursuing army's chariots.

The leader used his hand to free his people.

Exodus 14:21–22

The Solution

The Israelites were at the edge of the Red Sea. *Then Moses stretched out his hand over the sea, and all that night the LORD drove the sea back with a strong east wind and turned it into dry land. The waters were divided, and the Israelites went through the sea on dry ground, with a wall of water on their right and on their left. Exodus 14:21–22*

Bonus Question: What happened to Pharaoh's army after the Israelites crossed the Red Sea? (Exodus 14:29–30)

Bonus Answer: *The entire army drowned in the Red Sea.*

Bible Story: Exodus 13:17–22, 14:1–31

Discussion Questions:

1. What did the Israelites do when they saw the Egyptians marching after them? (Exodus 14:29–30)
   They became terrified, cried out to God, and began to question Moses.

2. How did Moses answer the people? (Exodus 14:13–14)
   He told them that they would never see the Egyptians again because the Lord would fight for them.

3. What happened when Moses stretched out his hand over the sea? (Exodus 14:26–28)
   The water covered the Egyptians.

The Prayer: Thank You, God, for Your strength and power. Thank You, for my salvation. Help us to have the faith of Moses. Amen.

CD-204023 *Tricky, Sticky Bible Riddles 2–3*

Name: _____

That day the LORD saved Israel from the hands of the Egyptians . . . .
Exodus 14:30

Directions: Decode the message to discover what happened after the Lord saved Israel from the Egyptians.
Check your answer by reading Exodus 14:31.

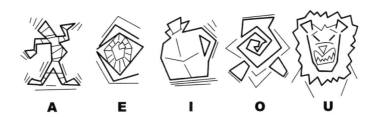

A   E   I   O   U

. . . wh__n th__ __sr____l__t__s s__w

_____ _____ _____

th__ gr__t p__w__r th__

_____ _____ _____ _____

L__RD d__spl__y__d __g__nst

_____ _____ _____

th__ __gypt__ns, th__ p__ __pl__ . . . .

_____ _____ _____

p__t th__r tr__st __n h__m

_____ _____ _____ _____

__nd __n M__s__s . . . .

_____ _____

Rude Awakening

The Riddle

The people of this city were awakened by loud sounds as foreigners rushed in and killed all of the town's inhabitants except for one family. In which city were almost all of the citizens killed?

The Clues

Music was played.

It took seven days for the city to be taken down.

The Lord gave the city to the attacking army to conquer.

Rahab's family was spared.

Joshua 6:1, 20–21

The Solution

Jericho *Now Jericho was tightly shut up because of the Israelites. No one went out and no one came in. . . . When the trumpets sounded, the people shouted, and at the sound of the trumpet, when the people gave a loud shout, the wall collapsed; so every man charged straight in, and they took the city. They devoted the city to the L*ORD *and destroyed with the sword every living thing in it . . . .*
Joshua 6:1, 20–21

Bonus Question: Who led the Israelites in overtaking Jericho? (Joshua 6:2)

Bonus Answer: *Joshua*

Bible Story: Joshua 5:13–6:27

Discussion Questions:

1. Whom did Joshua see as he drew near Jericho? (Joshua 5:13–15)
the commander of the Lord's army

2. What were God's instructions to overtake the city? (Joshua 6:2–5)
He wanted Joshua to march around the city with all of the armed men for six days, have seven priests carry trumpets of rams' horns in front of the ark, march around the city seven times on the seventh day with the priests blowing the trumpets, and have all of the people give a loud shout when the trumpet sounded.

3. What happened on the seventh day? (Joshua 6:20)
The walls came down, and Joshua and his people went into the city.

The Prayer: Dear God, Joshua listened to You. Help us to listen to Your teachings. Help us know right from wrong. Thank You for the Scriptures that give us directions, too. Amen.

Name:

On the seventh day, they got up at daybreak and marched around the city seven times in the same manner, except that on that day they circled the city seven times. Joshua 6:15

Directions: Solve the rebus to discover what Joshua said to his army. Check your answer by reading Joshua 6:16–17.

CD-204023 *Tricky, Sticky Bible Riddles 2–3*   © Carson-Dellosa

Defying Danger

Riddle #3

Where

The Riddle

Three faithful men walked in a place where no one had ever walked before. Where did the three men walk?

The Clues

It happened in Babylon.

The men were being punished by King Nebuchadnezzar.

The three men were tied up.

The place where they walked was very hot.

Daniel 3:25

The Solution

Shadrach, Meshach, and Abednego walked in a fiery furnace. *The king's command was so urgent and the furnace so hot that the flames of the fire killed the soldiers who took up Shadrach, Meshach and Abednego . . . . He said, "Look! I see four men walking around in the fire, unbound and unharmed, and the fourth looks like a son of the gods." Daniel 3:22, 25*

Bonus Question: Why were Shadrach, Meshach, and Abednego not afraid of the fiery furnace? (Daniel 3:16–17)

Bonus Answer: *They knew that God would save them.*

Bible Story: Daniel 3

Discussion Questions:

1. Why were Shadrach, Meshach, and Abednego thrown into the furnace? (Daniel 3:12)
   They didn't worship the king's idol.

2. What did the king see when he looked into the furnace? (Daniel 3:25)
   He saw four men walking in the fire.

3. How did the king reward Shadrach, Meshach, and Abednego? (Daniel 3:29–30)
   The king did not allow people to speak against God and he promoted the three men.

The Prayer: Dear Lord, even under the threat of death, Shadrach, Meshach, and Abednego were faithful to You. Help us to always be faithful to our beliefs and never be afraid to stand up for You. Amen.

46

© Carson-Dellosa

CD-204023 *Tricky, Sticky Bible Riddles 2–3*

Name: _____

It is my pleasure to tell you about the miraculous signs and wonders that the Most High God has performed for me. Daniel 4:2

Directions: Follow the directions below to reveal what King Nebuchadnezzar told his people. Check your answer by reading Daniel 4:3.

1. Change all of the Js to As.
2. Change all of the Bs to Es.
3. Change all of the Qs to Is.
4. Change all of the Vs to Os.
5. Change all of the Us to Ns.
6. Fill in the remaining letters.

Hvw   grbjt   jrb   hqs   sqgus,

____ ____ ____ ____ ____

hvw   maghty   hqs   wvudbrs!

____ ____ ____ ____

Hqs   kqugdvm   qs

____ ____ ____

ju   btbrujl   kqugdvm....

____ ____ ____

Riddle #4

No Escape

The Riddle

When a man tried to escape his calling and flee to this place, he almost caused many innocent men to lose their lives. Where was the man trying to flee?

The Clues

! The man was trying to run away from the Lord.

! A great storm arose.

! Sailors tried to determine who was responsible for the storm.

! They threw a man overboard.

! Jonah 1:3–4

The Solution

Tarshish *But Jonah ran away from the LORD and headed for Tarshish. He went down to Joppa, where he found a ship bound for that port. After paying the fare, he went aboard and sailed for Tarshish to flee from the LORD. Then the LORD sent a great wind on the sea, and such a violent storm arose that the ship threatened to break up.* Jonah 1:3–4

Bonus Question: What was Jonah doing when the storm began? (Jonah 1:5)

Bonus Answer: *He was sleeping.*

Bible Story: Jonah 1:1–2:10

Discussion Questions:

1. What did Jonah tell the men to do to him? (Jonah 1:12)
   to throw him into the sea

2. What happened immediately after the sailors threw Jonah overboard? (Jonah 1:15)
   The sea became calm.

3. What happened to Jonah when the men threw him into the sea? (Jonah 1:17)
   He was swallowed by a great fish.

The Prayer: Thank You, God, for Bible stories about Jonah and other people who chose, in the end, to obey You. Help us have the strength to do what is good and right and never think that we can run away or hide from You. Amen.

48

Name:

From inside the fish Jonah prayed to the LORD his God. Jonah 2:1

Directions: Decode the scrambled message and discover a part of Jonah's prayer. Check your answer by reading Jonah 2:9.

1. Change all of the Js to As.
2. Change all of the Bs to Es.
3. Change all of the Qs to Is.
4. Change all of the Zs to Os.
5. Change all of the Ys to Ws.
6. Fill in the remaining letters.

yhjt   q   hjvb   vzybd   q

_ _ _ _   _   _ _ _ _   _ _ _ _ _   _

yqll   mjkb   gzzd.   sjlvjtqzn

_ _ _ _   _ _ _ _   _ _ _ _.   _ _ _ _ _ _ _ _ _

czmbs   frzm   thb   Lzrd.

_ _ _ _ _   _ _ _ _   _ _ _   _ _ _ _.

Riddle #5

Disciples' Rude Deed

The Riddle

Three disciples disobeyed a direct request from Jesus. Where did the disciples do this thoughtless deed?

The Clues

Jesus asked the disciples to wait.

Jesus was sad and troubled.

Jesus went off to pray by himself.

After they disobeyed Him, Jesus said to the disciples, "The spirit is willing, but the body is weak."

Matthew 26:36, 38, 40

The Solution

They slept in the Garden of Gethsemane. *Then Jesus went with his disciples to a place called Gethsemane. Then he said to them. . . "Stay here. Keep watch with me." . . . Then he returned to his disciples and found them sleeping. . . .*
Matthew 26:36, 38, 40

Bonus Question: Why did Jesus leave the garden so suddenly? (Matthew 26:50)

Bonus Answer: *He was arrested and taken from the Garden of Gethsemane.*

Bible Story: Matthew 26:36–56

Discussion Questions:

1. How many times did Jesus pray in the garden? (Matthew 26:44)
   three times

2. How did Judas betray Jesus? (Matthew 26:48–49)
   with a kiss

3. When Jesus was arrested, what did the disciples do? (Matthew 26:56)
   They deserted Him.

The Prayer: Lord, Thank You, for sending Jesus to us. Help us to be strong when we feel weak. Help us to be faithful and not run away when we are faced with difficulty. Let us remember that through our struggles, we grow stronger. May we always remember that You hear our prayers and answer them. Amen.

 CD-204023 *Tricky, Sticky Bible Riddles 2–3*

Name:

At that time Jesus said to the crowd, "Am I leading a rebellion, that you have come out with swords and clubs to capture me?"
Matthew 26:55

Directions: Cross out the first letter and the last two letters to uncover why Jesus was arrested. The first one has been done for you. Check your answer by reading Matthew 26:56.

Scrambled	ANSWER:
X̶BUTX̶F̶	BUT
GTHISLE	_____
THASES	_____
ZALLJR	_____
XTAKENLY	_____
EPLACENT	_____
QTHATER	_____
YTHEWE	_____
MWRITINGSLY	_____
POFLY	_____
RTHEOK	_____
MPROPHETSOR	_____
NMIGHTER	_____
TBETE	_____
VFULFILLEDOB.	_____

CD-204023 *Tricky, Sticky Bible Riddles 2–3*

Desperate Travelers

The Riddle

A young family was forced to seek shelter in an undesirable place. During their stay, they were joined by visitors. Where was the undesirable shelter?

The Clues

It was in a town where a census was being taken.

The town was also called "the town of David."

Angels sang during the night.

The woman was pregnant.

Luke 2:15

The Solution

The undesirable shelter was in Bethlehem. *When the angels had left them and gone into heaven, the shepherds said to one another, "Let's go to Bethlehem and see this thing that has happened, which the Lord has told us about."* Luke 2:15

Bonus Question: What did the shepherds do after seeing the infant Jesus? (Luke 2:17)

Bonus Answer: *They told others about Him.*

Bible Story: Luke 2:1–20

Discussion Questions:

1. What did the angel say to the frightened shepherds? (Luke 2:10–12)
   The angel told them to not be afraid, that the Savior was born, and where they could find Him.

2. What did the angels sing? (Luke 2:14)
   "Glory to God in the highest, and on earth peace to men on whom his favor rests."

3. Where was Jesus lying when the shepherds saw Him? (Luke 2:16)
   in a manger

The Prayer: Thank You, God, for sending Jesus. Help us to not be fearful. We praise You and give glory to You in the highest. Amen.

CD-204023 *Tricky, Sticky Bible Riddles 2–3*

Name:

Suddenly a great company of the heavenly host appeared with the angel, praising God and saying . . . . Luke 2:13

Directions:

1. Photocopy this page.

2. Cut along the solid lines to cut out the scripture mat and word strips.

3. Fold the mat in half horizontally, centering the dotted lines. Cut a slit along each dotted line.

4. Weave the word strips together to see what the angels sang.

Scripture Mat

to	in	highest,
and	earth	to
whom	favor	Luke 2:14

Word Strips

| on | his | rests." |

| "Glory | God | the |

| on | peace | men |

CD-204023 *Tricky, Sticky Bible Riddles 2–3*

Lost Little Boy

The Riddle

A boy disappeared from His family. After searching for many days, His parents found Him. Where was the boy found?

The Clues

His parents were very worried.

The boy was 12–years–old.

Everyone who listened to the boy was amazed by what they heard.

The boy was surprised that His parents did not know where to find Him.

Luke 2:45–46

The Solution

Mary and Joseph found young Jesus in a Jerusalem temple. *When they did not find him, they went back to Jerusalem to look for him. After three days they found him in the temple courts, sitting among the teachers, listening to them and asking them questions.*
Luke 2:45–46

Bonus Question: What was Jesus doing when He was found? (Luke 2:46)

Bonus Answer: *He was sitting and talking with the religious teachers.*

Bible Story: Luke 2:41–52

Discussion Questions:

1. Where had Mary and Joseph been? (Luke 2:41)
   Jerusalem

2. How did Jesus' parents feel when they saw Him in the temple? (Luke 2:48)
   They were astonished.

3. What did Jesus ask His parents? (Luke 2:49)
   "Why were you searching for me? Didn't you know I had to be in my Father's house?"

The Prayer: Thank You, Lord, for giving us Your Son, who showed us how we should treat our parents. Help us always to be respectful and honor our parents as Jesus honored His. Amen.

CD-204023 *Tricky, Sticky Bible Riddles 2–3*

Then he went down to Nazareth with them and was obedient to them. But his mother treasured all these things in her heart. And Jesus grew in wisdom and stature, and in favor with God and men.
Luke 2:51–52

Directions: Jesus and His family traveled from their home in Nazareth to attend the Feast of the Passover in Jerusalem. Find the shortest route from Jerusalem to Nazareth.

CD-204023 *Tricky, Sticky Bible Riddles 2–3*   © Carson-Dellosa

Disappearing Diner

Riddle #8

The Riddle

A man ate and talked with friends and then vanished right before their eyes. Where were the friends gathered when the man disappeared?

The Clues

When the man arrived, the friends did not recognize him.

The man had been written about in the Old Testament Scriptures.

The man was Jesus, who was with His disciples.

Jesus was taken to heaven from this place.

Luke 24:50–51

The Solution

They were near Bethany.
When he led them out to the vicinity of Bethany, he lifted up his hands and blessed them. While he was blessing them, he left them and was taken up into heaven. Luke 24:50–51

Bonus Question: Where did the disciples go after Jesus ascended into heaven? (Luke 24:52–53)

Bonus Answer: *the Temple in Jerusalem*

Bible Story: Luke 24:36–53

Discussion Questions:

1. After Jesus was resurrected and came to His disciples, what did He say to them? (Luke 24:36)
"Peace be with you."

2. When the disciples first saw Jesus, what did they think? (Luke 24:37)
They thought that He was a ghost.

3. What did Jesus do to show the disciples that it was He? (Luke 24:40)
He showed them His hands and feet.

The Prayer: Thank You, God, for sending Jesus to earth, to die on the cross and rise again. We know that Your Son is in heaven with You. We are eager to do right in your eyes, just as Jesus did. Amen.

56

CD-204023 *Tricky, Sticky Bible Riddles 2–3*

Name:

Then he opened their minds so they could understand the Scriptures. Luke 24:45

Directions: Follow the directions below to reveal what Jesus told His disciples. Check your answer by reading Luke 24:46.

4 = C	21, 39 = N	1, 9, 31, 40, 43 = T
10 = W	29, 38 = O	2, 5, 32, 41, 44 = H
15 = U	8, 14, 25 = S	6, 19, 23, 28, 46 = R
30 = M	16, 17, 27 = F	22, 34, 37, 47, 48 = D
50 = Y	20, 36, 49 = A	3, 18, 26, 33, 35, 42 = E
12, 13 = L	7, 11, 24, 45 = I	

___ ___ ___   ___ ___ ___ ___ ___ ___
1   2   3   4   5   6   7   8   9

___ ___ ___ ___   ___ ___ ___ ___ ___ ___
10 11 12 13   14 15 16 17 18 19

___ ___ ___   ___ ___ ___ ___   ___ ___ ___ ___
20 21 22   23 24 25 26   27 28 29 30

___ ___ ___   ___ ___ ___ ___   ___ ___
31 32 33   34 35 36 37   38 39

___ ___ ___   ___ ___ ___ ___ ___   ___ ___ ___
40 41 42   43 44 45 46 47   48 49 50

Miraculous Career Begins

The Riddle

At a gathering of friends and family, a mother told her Son to do something. He objected at first, but He later did as she asked, which launched a miraculous career. Where did this miraculous event take place?

The Clues

People were celebrating.

Jesus' mother, Mary, was there.

Water was not usually served at these celebrations.

Jesus performed His first miracle.

John 2:1, 11

The Solution

It took place at a wedding at Cana in Galilee. *On the third day a wedding took place at Cana in Galilee . . . . This, the first of his miraculous signs, Jesus performed in Cana in Galilee . . . .* John 2:1, 11

Bonus Question: Who else accompanied Jesus to the wedding? (John 2:2)

Bonus Answer: His disciples

Bible Story: John 2:1–11

Discussion Questions:

1. What did Jesus' mother tell the servants to do? (John 2:5)
   to do whatever Jesus told them to do

2. What did Jesus tell the servants to do? (John 2:8)
   to fill the jars with water and to take some to the master of the banquet

3. After witnessing the miracle, how did the disciples react? (John 2:11)
   They put their faith in Him.

The Prayer: Thank You, God, for the example that Jesus set as a man who honored His mother. Thank You for our mothers, who love us and take care of us. Help us remember to do as Jesus did, and always listen to, obey, and love our mothers. Amen.

Name:

Nearby stood six stone water jars, the kind used by the Jews for ceremonial washing, each holding from twenty to thirty gallons.
John 2:6

Directions: Decode the message to discover why Jesus performed His first miracle. Check your answer by reading John 2:11.

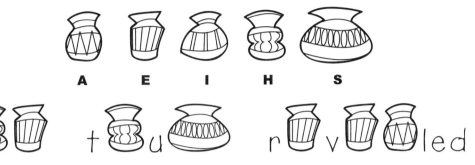

A   E   I   H   S

 tu r v led

_____   _____   _____

 glory, nd

_____

 dc pl put

_____   _____   ____

tr f t n m.

_____   _____   ____   ____

Something Missing

Riddle #1

The Riddle

A lonely man awoke and found that while he had slept, he had lost something but had gained something else. Why did the man feel like he had lost and also found something?

The Clues

The man took a long nap.

Something new was made.

It happened in a garden.

The man was no longer lonely.

Genesis 2:21–22

The Solution

While Adam was sleeping, God removed one of his ribs and made a woman. *So the LORD God caused the man to fall into a deep sleep; and while he was sleeping, he took one of the man's ribs and closed up the place with flesh. Then the LORD God made a woman from the rib he had taken out of the man, and he brought her to the man.* Genesis 2:21–22

Bonus Question: What did Adam say "woman" means? (Genesis 2:23)

Bonus Answer: *taken out of man*

Bible Story: Genesis 2:19–24

Discussion Questions:

1. What job did God give Adam? (Genesis 2:19)
   to name all of the animals

2. What was Adam trying to find? (Genesis 2:20)
   a suitable helper

3. What did Adam say when he saw Eve? (Genesis 2:23)
   "This is now bone of my bones and flesh of my flesh; she shall be called 'woman,' for she was taken out of man."

The Prayer: Thank You, God, for our families and friends, who keep us company. Help us to be suitable helpers to our friends and families. Amen.

CD-204023 *Tricky, Sticky Bible Riddles 2–3*

So the man gave names to all the livestock, the birds of the air and all the beasts of the field. . . . Genesis 2:20

Directions: Find 36 different animals hidden in the word search. Words can be found up, down, forward, backward, and diagonally.

alligator	butterfly	dog	hen	pig	sloth
bat	cheetah	fish	horse	raccoon	snail
bear	camel	fox	lamb	rat	squirrel
beaver	cat	frog	lion	seal	toucan
bird	cow	giraffe	mule	shark	wolf
bug	deer	gorilla	panther	skunk	worm

```
o  i  l  k  m  b  u  s  e  c  p  p  o  a  g  f  p
o  e  a  e  u  u  x  q  o  a  x  o  i  l  x  v  a
c  a  m  e  l  g  b  u  t  t  e  r  f  l  y  y  n
z  x  b  x  e  e  p  i  g  i  e  b  g  i  x  i  t
w  o  r  m  x  s  f  r  o  g  i  e  o  g  x  k  h
b  s  h  a  r  k  x  r  m  x  x  a  r  a  t  i  e
e  g  i  r  a  f  f  e  b  s  x  r  i  t  e  n  r
a  x  n  x  c  a  d  l  e  h  e  n  l  o  l  i  j
v  t  o  u  c  a  n  t  r  a  t  e  l  r  e  o  n
e  r  x  d  o  g  x  y  x  r  d  x  a  x  p  p  t
r  x  x  o  x  h  s  s  k  u  n  k  x  h  m  x  y
r  a  c  s  n  a  i  l  n  s  c  x  l  y  a  n  r
s  n  a  l  d  x  p  p  a  e  k  x  f  e  n  b  a
d  e  e  r  x  f  p  i  k  a  w  a  g  t  t  v  c
b  a  t  g  l  i  o  n  e  l  v  a  f  o  x  q  c
c  f  r  t  y  r  w  q  o  p  x  b  h  i  i  r  o
c  h  e  e  t  a  h  u  n  m  w  o  l  f  x  y  o
d  j  r  x  l  q  t  w  i  f  m  o  o  q  h  t  n
b  i  r  d  v  z  o  q  e  s  k  h  c  l  j  y  z
h  s  i  f  x  y  l  u  o  n  g  e  q  m  z  p  f
z  e  q  l  a  e  s  h  x  g  h  o  r  s  e  t  c
```

CD-204023 *Tricky, Sticky Bible Riddles 2–3*

Riddle #2

Stocking Up

The Riddle

For seven years, a man stored up so much food that he couldn't even keep track of all of it. Why did the man collect such huge quantities of food?

The Clues

It happened in Egypt.

The man was second in command.

The seven years of abundance came to an end.

The man who saved food was known to some by the name Zaphenath-Paneah.

Genesis 41:48–49

The Solution

Joseph was collecting food while it was plentiful so that it would be available during times of famine. *Joseph collected all the food produced in those seven years of abundance in Egypt and stored it in the cities. . . . Joseph stored up huge quantities of grain, like the sand of the sea; it was so much that he stopped keeping records because it was beyond measure.*
Genesis 41:48–49

Bonus Question: What did Joseph end up doing with all of the food? (Genesis 41:54–57)

Bonus Answer: *During the seven-year famine, he fed the Egyptians and people from surrounding countries.*

Bible Story: Genesis 41

Discussion Questions:

1. What convinced Pharaoh to put Joseph in charge of collecting food? (Genesis 41:39–40)
   No one was as discerning and wise as Joseph.

2. Why did Joseph stop keeping records of the food that was stored? (Genesis 41:49)
   There was too much food to count.

3. What did Pharaoh tell his people to do when the famine came? (Genesis 41:55)
   to go to Joseph

The Prayer: Lord, help us pay attention to Your voice. Help us to know what we should do to be helpful to and loving of others. Amen.

CD-204023 *Tricky, Sticky Bible Riddles 2–3*

Name: _____

Then Pharaoh said to Joseph, "In my dream I was standing on the bank of the Nile . . . ." Genesis 41:17

Directions: Decode the message to discover more about Pharaoh's dream. Check your answer by reading Genesis 41:18–19.

F A M I N E

"...whO𝗟 out o🐸 thO r◇vOr

_____ _____

thOrO c🍎🥊O up sOvO𝗟 cows,

_____ _____

🐸🍎t 🍎𝗟d slOOk, 🍎𝗟d thOy

_____ _____

gr🍎zOd 🍎🥊o𝗟g thO rOOds.

_____

🍎🐸tOr thO🥊, sOvO𝗟

_____ _____

othOr cows c🍎🥊O up-scr🍎w𝗟y

_____ _____

🍎𝗟d vOry ugly 🍎𝗟d lO🍎𝗟...."

_____

CD-204023 *Tricky, Sticky Bible Riddles 2–3*

© Carson-Dellosa

One Angry Man

The Riddle

The sight of an object angered a man so much that he destroyed it in front of a crowd who really liked the object. Why did the sight of something make the man angry?

The Clues

The man hadn't eaten for 40 days.

The people who liked the object were called "stiff-necked."

The object was in the shape of an animal.

The man burned, crushed, and ground up the object and then threw it into a stream.

Deuteronomy 9:21

The Solution

The Israelites were worshiping a golden calf, which Moses destroyed. "*Also I took that sinful thing of yours, the calf you had made, and burned it in the fire. Then I crushed it and ground it to powder as fine as dust and threw the dust into a stream that flowed down the mountain.*" Deuteronomy 9:21

Bonus Question: What had Moses brought from God to His people? (Deuteronomy 9:10)

Bonus Answer: *He brought the Ten Commandments.*

Bible Story: Deuteronomy 9:1–21

Discussion Questions:

1. Besides Moses, who was angry at the Israelites for their displays of rebellion? (Deuteronomy 9:7)
   God

2. What did Moses not do for 40 days and nights? (Deuteronomy 9:9)
   eat or drink

3. What did Moses do with the first set of tablets? (Deuteronomy 9:17)
   He threw them and broke them.

The Prayer: Thank You, Father, for the Ten Commandments. Thank You for the Bible that teaches us right from wrong. Help us to not stray from Your commandments the way the Israelites did. Amen.

CD-204023 *Tricky, Sticky Bible Riddles 2–3*

And God spoke all these words: "I am the LORD your God, who brought you out of Egypt, out of the land of slavery." Exodus 20:1–2

Directions: Unscramble the Ten Commandments.

oYu halls avhe on rothe dgos reebfo em.

_____

Yuo halls ton kame soidl.

_____

oYu sllha nto muisse hte amne fo hte rLod ouyr Gdo.

_____

Rbermeme eth Sbathab nad peek ti lohy.

_____

onHor yrou athfer dan yrou thmoer.

_____

ouY halls ton mdeurr.

_____

ouY sallh tno citmom dulatery.

_____

oYu sallh otn salte.

_____

uYo halls tno ivge alfse ttyimeson.

_____

oYu sllha tno ceovt yrou nbogheir's oushe.

_____

CD-204023 *Tricky, Sticky Bible Riddles 2–3*

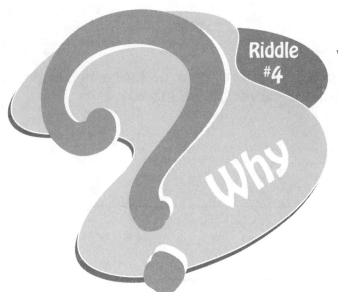

Going Hungry

The Riddle

A woman was responsible for many of her people going hungry for three days and nights while she prepared a banquet for another. Why did the woman have so many go hungry while she prepared a feast for another?

The Clues

The woman's people were the Jewish people.

The woman was a queen.

The queen was raised by her cousin Mordecai.

The queen's cousin wouldn't bow down to the king's administrator.

Esther 4:15–16

The Solution

Queen Esther asked all of her people to fast for three days and night. *Then Esther sent this reply to Mordecai: "Go, gather together all the Jews who are in Susa, and fast for me. Do not eat or drink for three days, night or day. I and my maids will fast as you do. When this is done, I will go to the king, even though it is against the law. And if I perish, I perish." Esther 4:15–16*

Bonus Question: Why did Queen Esther prepare a banquet for her husband? (Esther 5)

Bonus Answer: *She prepared a banquet so that she could petition him to save her people.*

Bible Story: Esther 3–5

Discussion Questions:

1. What were the king's orders that so disturbed Esther? (Esther 3:12–15)
to kill all of the Jewish people

2. Why was it potentially dangerous to approach the king? (Esther 4:10–11)
One could be put to death for approaching the king without being summoned.

3. What did Esther do on the third day? (Esther 5:1–4)
She went to the king.

The Prayer: Thank You, God, for the strong women in our lives. Thank You for women like Queen Esther who love us, want to protect us from harm, and will stand up for us. Amen.

CD-204023 *Tricky, Sticky Bible Riddles 2–3*

Name: _____

For the Jews it was a time of happiness and joy, gladness and honor. Esther 8:16

Directions: Read Esther 8:17. Find and circle the words below that can be found in the verse. Answers can be found up, down, across, forward, backward, and diagonally.

celebrating	every	joy
city	feasting	Jews
edict	gladness	king

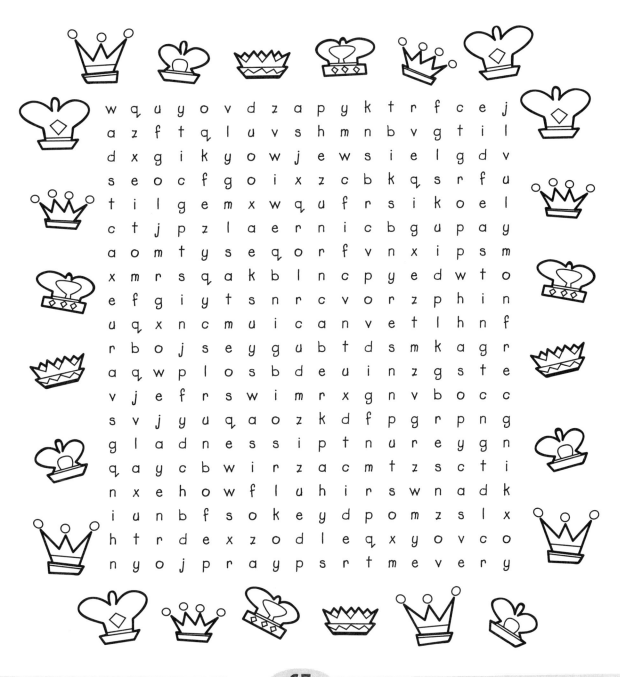

```
w q u y o v d z a p y k t r f c e j
a z f t q l u v s h m n b v g t i l
d x g i k y o w j e w s i e l g d v
s e o c f g o i x z c b k q s r f u
t i l g e m x w q u f r s i k o e l
c t j p z l a e r n i c b g u p a y
a o m t y s e q o r f v n x i p s m
x m r s q a k b l n c p y e d w t o
e f g i y t s n r c v o r z p h i n
u q x n c m u i c a n v e t l h n f
r b o j s e y g u b t d s m k a g r
a q w p l o s b d e u i n z g s t e
v j e f r s w i m r x g n v b o c c
s v j y u q a o z k d f p g r p n g
g l a d n e s s i p t n u r e y g n
q a y c b w i r z a c m t z s c t i
n x e h o w f l u h i r s w n a d k
i u n b f s o k e y d p o m z s l x
h t r d e x z o d l e q x y o v c o
n y o j p r a y p s r t m e v e r y
```

CD-204023 *Tricky, Sticky Bible Riddles 2–3*

One King for Another

The Riddle

Some men defied a king's orders by withholding important information from him. Why did the men defy the king?

The Clues

It began in Jerusalem.

The king was looking for something.

The men found what the king wanted.

The men gave three very nice gifts.

Matthew 2:8, 12

The Solution

In a dream, God warned the wise men to not return to the king or tell him where he could find Jesus. *He sent them to Bethlehem and said, "Go and make a careful search for the child. As soon as you find him, report to me, so that I too may go and worship him." . . . And having been warned in a dream not to go back to Herod, they returned to their country by another route.* Matthew 2:8, 12

Bonus Question: How did the wise men know how to find Jesus? (Matthew 2:9)

Bonus Answer: *A star led them.*

Bible Story: Matthew 2:1–15

Discussion Questions:

1. What was the name of the group of wise men? (Matthew 2:1)
   Magi

2. How did King Herod know that Jesus would be born in Bethlehem? (Matthew 2:5–6)
   The chief priests and teachers of the law told Herod that this had been written by the prophets.

3. What was the reason the king gave for wanting to see Jesus? (Matthew 2:8)
   to worship Him

The Prayer: Thank You, God, for the first Christmas. Thank You for sending Jesus—the bright and shining star. When we see the first bright star each night, help us to remember that You sent Your Son to earth to give us light and save us from our sins.

CD-204023 *Tricky, Sticky Bible Riddles 2–3*

Name:

On coming to the house, they saw the child with his mother Mary. . . .
Matthew 2:11

Directions: Look up Matthew 2:11 and fill in the crossword grid using the words below. One word has been filled in for you.

bowed	gold	myrrh	treasures
down	him	opened	worshiped
gifts	incense	presented	

Riddle #6

Why

Sudden Cries

The Riddle

A man heard a rather noisy bird, which made him cry. Why did the sound of the bird make the man cry?

The Clues

The occurrence had been predicted.

It happened in the high priest's courtyard.

The crying man said, "I don't know the man!"

The man lied three times.

Matthew 26:74–75

The Solution

Jesus had predicted that before the rooster crowed, Peter would deny that he knew Him three times.

. . . Immediately a rooster crowed. Then Peter remembered the word Jesus had spoken: "Before the rooster crows, you will disown me three times." And he went outside and wept bitterly.
Matthew 26:74–75

Bonus Question: Besides Peter, which disciple betrayed Jesus in this Bible story? (Matthew 26:47–49)

Bonus Answer: *Judas*

Bible Story: Matthew 26:31–75

Discussion Questions:

1. What did Peter declare when Jesus told him he would deny Jesus three times? (Matthew 26:35)
   that he would never disown Jesus

2. When the girl said "This fellow was with Jesus of Nazareth," what did Peter do? (Matthew 26:72)
   He denied knowing Jesus.

3. When it was said that Peter's accent gave him away what did Peter do? (Matthew 26:74)
   He said "I don't know the man!"

The Prayer: Thank You, Lord, for my country where I do not have to hide my love for You. Please help us to never deny You or be ashamed to tell others about You. Amen.

CD-204023 *Tricky, Sticky Bible Riddles 2–3*

Peter replied, "Even if all fall away on account of you, I never will."
Matthew 26:33

Directions: Solve the rebus puzzle to discover what Jesus told His disciples at the Passover meal. Check your answer by reading Matthew 26:34.

"   TELL   THE

_____   _____   _____   _____

TRUTH,"   ANSWERED,

_____   _____   _____

"THIS   V+  -B-R   ,   B 4

_____   _____   _____   _____

THE       ,   WILL

_____   _____   _____   _____

DISOWN    -N   3    +S."

_____   _____   _____   _____

Laughing Mourners

The Riddle

Jesus said something that made a group of mourners laugh—but it was not a joke. Why did the mourners laugh at what Jesus said?

The Clues

! It happened in the home of the synagogue ruler.

! The ruler's daughter died.

! Three disciples were with Jesus.

! Jesus asked, "Why all this commotion and wailing?"

! Mark 5:39–40

The Solution

They laughed because Jesus said that the girl was sleeping and they knew her to be dead. *He went in and said to them, "Why all this commotion and wailing? The child is not dead but asleep." But they laughed at him. . . .*
Mark 5:39–40

Bonus Question: What happened after the people laughed at Jesus? (Mark 5:40–42)

Bonus Answer: *He sent the mourners out, took the girl by the hand, and told the girl to get up, which she did.*

Bible Story: Mark 5:35–43

Discussion Questions:

1. Whom did Jesus take with Him when He went to the synagogue ruler's house? (Mark 5:37)
   Peter, James, and John

2. How old was the girl? (Mark 5:42)
   twelve

3. What orders did Jesus give the people after the girl was revived? (Mark 5:43)
   not to tell anyone

The Prayer: Thank You, God, for caring for every single person. We love You. We want to do what is right. Help our faith grow as we grow and let us become all that we can be in Your name. Amen.

 CD-204023 *Tricky, Sticky Bible Riddles 2–3*

While Jesus was still speaking, some men came from the house of Jairus, the synagogue ruler. "Your daughter is dead," they said. "Why bother the teacher any more?" Mark 5:35

Directions: Look up Mark 5:36 to find out what Jesus told Jairus not to be. Fit the keyword from Jesus' command in the number-letter grid below. The first letter has been done for you.

Letter 2: Connect E1 to E10. Connect E1 to H1. Connect E5 to H5.

Letter 3: Connect I1 to I10. Connect I1 to L1. Connect L1 to I5. Connect I5 to L6. Connect L6 to L10.

Letter 4: Connect M1 to M10. Connect M1 to P1. Connect P1 to P10. Connect M5 to P5.

Letter 5: Connect Q1 to U1. Connect Q10 to U10. Connect S1 to S10.

Letter 6: Connect V1 to V10. Connect V1 to Z3. Connect Z3 to Z9. Connect Z9 to V10.

CD-204023 *Tricky, Sticky Bible Riddles 2–3*

Riddle #8

Muddy-Faced Man

The Riddle

After washing his muddy face, a man happily lost his job. Why did the man have to find a new career after having mud on his face?

The Clues

It happened in the Pool of Siloam.

Mud had been placed on the man's eyes by another person.

After washing his face, his neighbors did not think that he was the same person.

Jesus helped the man.

John 9:6–7

The Solution

Jesus made mud and gave a blind beggar sight. *Having said this, he spit on the ground, made some mud with the saliva, and put it on the man's eyes. "Go," he told him, "wash in the Pool of Siloam" (this word means Sent). So the man went and washed, and came home seeing.*
John 9:6–7

Bonus Question: What did the disciples believe had caused the man's blindness? (John 9:2)

Bonus Answer: *They thought that he had been punished for either his or his parents' sins.*

Bible Story: John 9:1–12

Discussion Questions:

1. What was the blind man's former occupation? (John 9:8)
   He was a beggar.

2. After putting mud on the blind man's eyes, what was the man told to do? (John 9:7)
   to wash in the Pool of Siloam

3. When people asked the man how he had been healed, what did he tell them? (John 9:11)
   that Jesus put mud on his eyes and told him to wash in the Pool of Siloam

The Prayer: Thank You, God, for sending Your Son, Jesus, to be the light of the world. Help us to do good in Your sight. Help us not to be blind to the truth. Amen.

   CD-204023 *Tricky, Sticky Bible Riddles 2–3*

Name:

As long as it is day, we must do the work of him who sent me. . . .
John 9:4

Directions: Use the code to decode Jesus' message to His disciples. Check your answer by reading John 9:5.

A	C	D
E	F	G
H	I	J

K	L	M
N	O	R
S	T	W

W H I L E

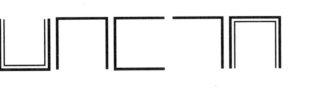

In No Hurry to Heal

The Riddle

A healer, who was in no hurry, was too late to prevent a man from dying. Why didn't the healer hurry to save the dying man?

The Clues

It happened in Bethany.

A short while before the death of the man, some people had tried to stone the healer.

The man had been dead for four days.

The dead man's sisters were Mary and Martha.

John 11:4

The Solution

Jesus wanted the opportunity to demonstrate the glory of God. . . . *Jesus said, "This sickness will not end in death. No, it is for God's glory so that God's Son may be glorified through it."* John 11:4

Bonus Question: What happened to Lazarus, who had been dead for four days? (John 11:43–44)

Bonus Answer: *At Jesus' command, Lazarus was brought back to life.*

Bible Story: John 11:1–45

Discussion Questions:

1. What did Jesus find when he arrived at Lazarus' home? (John 11:17)
   Lazarus had already been in the tomb for four days.

2. How did Martha demonstrate her faith in Jesus? (John 11:21–22, 27)
   She told Him that she believed that He was the Son of God and that God would give Him what He asked.

3. What happened as a result of Lazarus' healing? (John 11:45)
   The Jewish people began to put their faith in Him.

The Prayer: Heavenly Father, Mary and Martha loved their brother, Lazarus. Thank You for families and making them a part of Your plan for us. Help us to love our families the way that Mary and Martha loved their brother. Amen.

CD-204023 *Tricky, Sticky Bible Riddles 2–3*

Name:

Jesus said to her, "I am the resurrection and the life . . . ."
John 11:25

Directions: Unscramble the words to discover something important that Jesus told Martha. Check your answer by reading John 11:25–26.

"...eH how ebleeivs ni em liwl vile,

_____ _____ _____ _____ _____ _____ _____ _____

veen hothug eh side; dan roevewh

_____ _____ _____ _____ _____ _____

sivle nad vebeelis ni

_____ _____ _____ _____

em lilw reven ide...."

_____ _____ _____ _____ _____

Answer Key

Page 7 . . . that you may know that I am the Lord.

Page 9 That evening quail came and covered the camp, and in the morning there was a layer of dew around the camp.

Page 11 the battle is the Lord's . . . .

Page 13 . . . because they saw that he had wisdom from God to administer justice.

Page 15 FATHER

Page 17

Page 19 This is my Son, whom I love; with him I am well pleased.

Page 21 PEACE

Page 23 "You will always have the poor among you, but you will not always have me." John 12:8

Page 25 Cursed is the ground because of you; through painful toil you will eat of it all the days of your life.

Page 27
Adam lived 930 years.
Seth lived 912 years.
Enosh lived 905 years.
Kenan lived 910 years.
Mahalalel lived 895 years.
Jared lived 962 years.
Enoch lived 365 years.
Methuselah lived 969 years.
Lamech lived 777 years.
Noah lived 950 years.

Page 29 The bat, snake, and turtle do not have a mate.

Page 31 Will your mother and I and your brothers actually come and bow down to the ground before you?

Page 33
1—Matthew 2:2	4—Psalm 104:4	7— Psalm 104:3
2—Psalm 51:7	5—Genesis 7:12	8—Genesis 1:14
3—Exodus 9:23	6—Psalm 93:4	

Page 35 "You of little faith," he said, "why did you doubt?"

Page 37 "We have seen remarkable things today."

CD-204023 *Tricky, Sticky Bible Riddles 2–3*

Answer Key

Page 39 "Because this man, too, is a son of Abraham. For the Son of Man came to seek and to save what was lost."

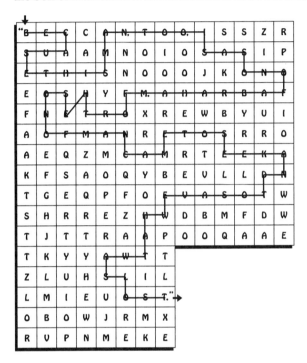

Page 41 "Surely this is the Prophet who is to come into the world."

Page 43 ... when the Israelites saw the great power the Lord displayed against the Egyptians, the people... put their trust in him and in Moses ....

Page 45 The seventh time around, when the priests sounded the trumpet blast, Joshua commanded the people, "Shout! For the Lord has given you the city! The city and all that is in it are to be devoted to the Lord."

Page 47 How great are his signs, how mighty his wonders! His kingdom is an eternal kingdom ....

Page 49 What I have vowed I will make good. Salvation comes from the Lord.

Page 51 But this has all taken place that the writings of the prophets might be fulfilled.

Page 53 "Glory to God in the highest, and on earth peace to men on whom his favor rests." Luke 2:14

Page 55

Page 57 The Christ will suffer and rise from the dead on the third day

Page 59 He thus revealed his glory, and his disciples put their faith in him.

Page 61

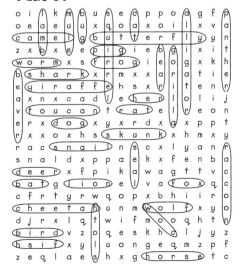

Answer Key

Page 63 . . . when out of the river there came up seven cows, fat and sleek, and they grazed among the reeds. After them, seven other cows came up—scrawny and very ugly and lean. . . .

Page 65

1. You shall have no other gods before me.
2. You shall not make idols.
3. You shall not misuse the name of the Lord your God.
4. Remember the Sabbath and keep it holy.
5. Honor your father and your mother.
6. You shall not murder.
7. You shall not commit adultery.
8. You shall not steal.
9. You shall not give false testimony.
10. You shall not covet your neighbor's house.

Page 67

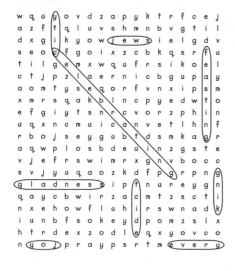

Page 69

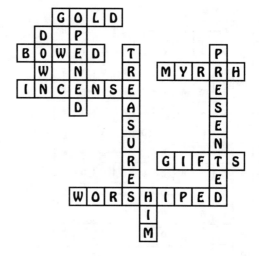

Page 71 "I tell you the truth," Jesus answered, "this very night, before the rooster crows, you will disown me three times."

Page 73 AFRAID

Page 75 While I am in the world, I am the light of the world.

Page 77 He who believes in me will live, even though he dies; and whoever lives and believes in me will never die . . . .

© Carson-Dellosa   CD-204023 *Tricky, Sticky Bible Riddles 2–3*